Horse Crafts

Written and Illustrated by
Linda Hendry

KIDS CAN PRESS

For my horse-loving cousins

Text and illustrations © 2006 Linda Hendry

KIDS CAN DO IT and the 🖍 logo are trademarks of Kids Can Press Ltd.

Kids Can Press acknowledges the financial support of the Government of Ontario, through the Ontario Media Development Corporation's Ontario Book Initiative, and the Government of Canada, through the BPIDP, for our publishing activity.

Published in Canada by	Published in the U.S. by
Kids Can Press Ltd	Kids Can Press Ltd.
29 Birch Avenue	2250 Military Road
Toronto, ON M4V 1E2	Tonawanda, NY 14150

www.kidscanpress.com

Edited by Laurie Wark
Designed by Kathleen Collett
Photography by Frank Baldassarra
Printed and bound in China

The hardcover edition of this book is smyth sewn casebound.
The paperback edition of this book is limp sewn with a drawn-on cover.

CM 06 0 9 8 7 6 5 4 3 2 1
CM PA 06 0 9 8 7 6 5 4 3 2 1

Library and Archives Canada Cataloguing in Publication

Hendry, Linda
Horse crafts / written and illustrated by Linda Hendry.

(Kids can do it)
ISBN-13: 978-1-55337-646-0 (bound).   ISBN-13: 978-1-55337-647-7 (pbk.)
ISBN-10: 1-55337-646-3 (bound).   ISBN-10: 1-55337-647-1 (pbk.)

1. Handicraft — Juvenile literature. 2. Horses — Juvenile literature.
I. Title. II. Series.

TT160.H399 2006   j745.5   C2004-907188-2

Kids Can Press is a *corus*™ Entertainment company

12/07

Contents

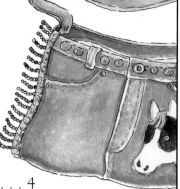

Introduction and materials 4

Sewing 6

Draw a horse 8

Make a silhouette 10

Pony pencil pal 12

Sunset shade 14

Pony pin 16

Browband cover 18

Paddock mirror 20

Pony plaque 22

Clippity-clop clipboard 24

Pasture pillow 26

Horsin' around keepsake box 28

Blue jean bag 30

Bronco bookend 32

CD stable 34

Sock horse 36

Patterns 39

Introduction

Whether you own a horse, take riding lessons at a stable or just love horses from afar, you'll have a galloping good time making the horse-themed crafts in this book. Make a browband cover for your horse's bridle and a matching scrunchee for your hair. Turn clothespins and cardboard into a clippity-clop clipboard to hang in your room. Or turn a pair of wooly work socks into a wonderful pony pal! This book will show you how. Giddyap! Let's go!

MATERIALS

These crafts are made from easy-to-find materials you probably have around your home. A craft supply store should have the materials you need to buy. Before you glue or paint, cover your work surface with newspaper to protect it.

Cardboard

Some projects require corrugated cardboard or light cardboard. Corrugated cardboard is used to make boxes for heavy things. Ask your grocer for a box. For light cardboard you can use cracker or cereal boxes.

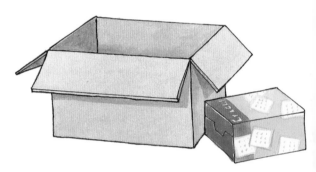

Glue

White, non-toxic glue is strong and dries clear. Clothespins can often be used to hold pieces together until the glue is dry.

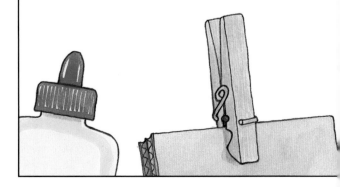

Scissors and utility knives

Most cutting can be done with a pair of sharp scissors. Small, pointy scissors are good for cutting out silhouettes. When you would like a straighter edge, use a utility knife and a metal-edged ruler.

For some crafts you need to score along a fold line. To do this, lay a metal-edged ruler along the fold line and make a very light cut along the edge of the ruler with a utility knife. Do not cut completely through the cardboard. Always ask an adult to help you use a utility knife, and protect your work surface with a piece of corrugated cardboard.

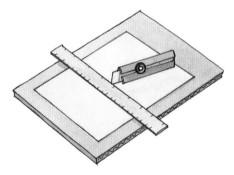

Paints and brushes

Acrylic craft paints are bright and colorful and give your project a smooth finish. They dry fast, so pour only as much as you need onto a piece of waxed paper. Use small, pointed brushes for painting details, and flat, straight-edged brushes for painting large areas. Clean your brushes with water between each color, and rinse them well when you are finished painting.

Collage

You'll use a collage technique to make several crafts in this book.

1 Mix 4 spoonfuls of white glue with 2 spoonfuls of water in a plastic container.

2 Use a paintbrush to spread the glue mixture onto a small area of your project.

3 Apply pieces of paper or photos to the wet areas and smooth them out with the brush. Wrap the pieces neatly around any edges. Continue until your project is covered.

4 Brush on a final layer of glue mixture to seal the paper or photos.

Sewing

You'll need to do some basic sewing for some of the crafts. Check these pages when you need help with the stitches.

Start with a piece of thread about twice the length of your arm. Wet one end of the thread and poke it through the eye of the needle. Pull the ends even and knot the double end.

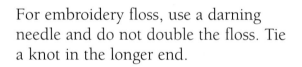

For embroidery floss, use a darning needle and do not double the floss. Tie a knot in the longer end.

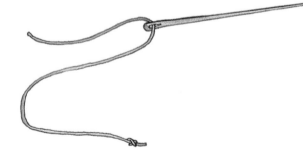

When you finish sewing or run out of thread, make several small stitches near the last stitch and cut the thread.

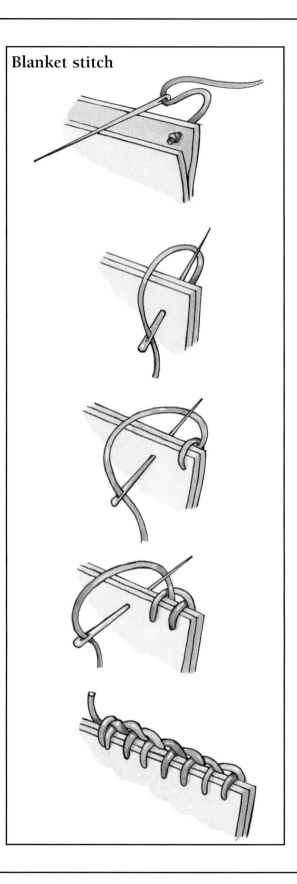

Blanket stitch

Overcast stitch

Backstitch

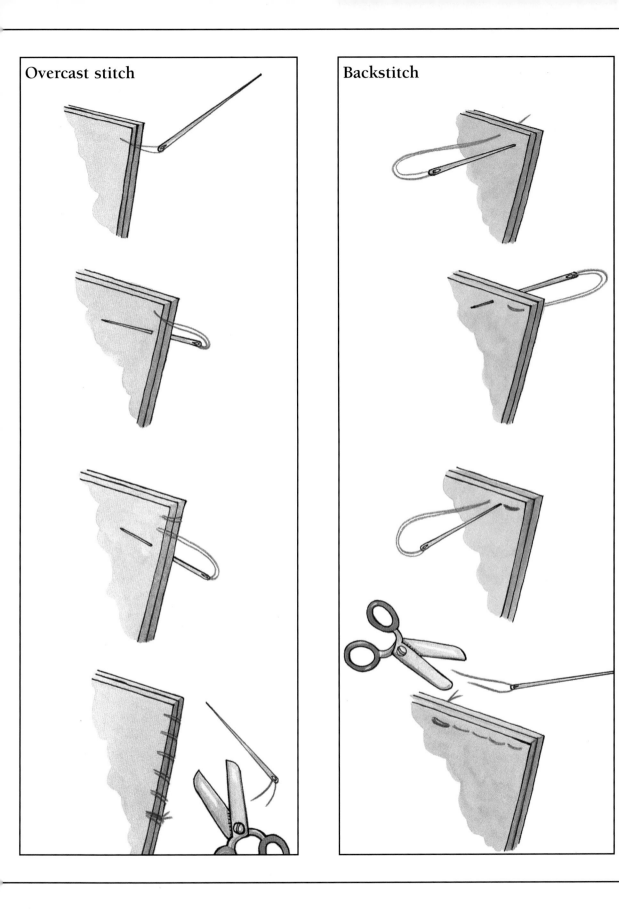

Draw a horse

These instructions will have you drawing horses in no time. Studying photos or watching horses will help you perfect your drawing skills.

YOU WILL NEED

- paper
- a pencil, an eraser
- tracing paper
- colored pencils, watercolors or pastels (optional)

1 On the paper, draw a jellybean shape for a ribcage and a squished balloon shape for a rump.

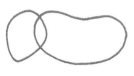

2 Add a curved neck line and draw a line along the back.

3 Draw a ball for a cheek and a smaller ball for a nose. Join the balls to create the face.

4 Estimate how long the horse's legs will be, and draw a ground line.

5 Draw a ball for the hip joint.

6 Draw a ball where each leg joins the body. (Think of this joint as your shoulder joint.) Draw a line to join the hip joint to the shoulder joint.

7 The next joints work like your elbow or knee. Draw a line to connect these joints to the shoulder joints.

8 The next joints are like your wrists. Join them to the knee and elbow joints.

9 The last joints are like the knuckles at the ends of your fingers. Join them to the wrist joints.

10 Lay tracing paper over your layout and sketch out your horse, making any changes you like. When you are happy with your drawing, trace it onto paper or make some photocopies of it. Try coloring them with colored pencils, watercolors or pastels.

Make a silhouette

Use your finished silhouettes to decorate some of the projects in this book. You can also photocopy them onto different-colored papers and make greeting cards or frame them to make great gifts.

YOU WILL NEED

- photos or pictures of horses
- tracing paper
- thin and thick black felt markers
- white and colored paper (optional)

1 Choose a photo or picture of a horse. Side views work best.

2 Lay a sheet of tracing paper over the picture and trace around the horse with the thin marker. If you want, add a ground line, background details or a border.

3 Remove the picture and start filling in the horse. Use the thin marker to color small areas and the wide marker for large areas until you have a solid black silhouette.

4 Photocopy the silhouette, reducing or enlarging it as you like. Make as many copies as you need for your project.

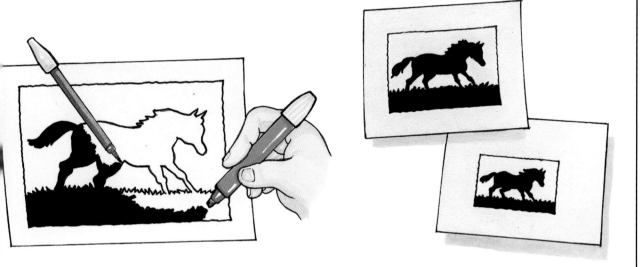

MORE IDEAS

To make greeting cards, center the silhouette on the lower half of a sheet of white letter-size paper and use clear tape to hold it in place. Photocopy the image onto different-colored sheets of card stock, then score a fold line along the centre of each sheet and fold it back to make a card.

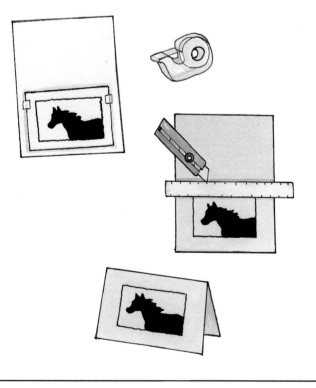

Pony pencil pal

Turn a glove into a stable full of colorful ponies for you and your friends!

YOU WILL NEED

- a lightweight, stretchy knit glove
- a small piece of fiberfill stuffing
- a pencil
- embroidery floss or yarn in 3 colors
- a scrap of felt
- 2 small craft eyes
- scissors, a needle and thread, glue, a thin black felt marker

1 Cut off a finger of the glove at the base.

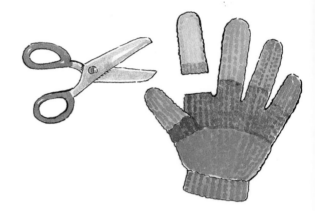

2 Stuff the finger half full with fiberfill stuffing, then push the eraser end of the pencil halfway into the finger.

3 Tightly wrap a piece of embroidery floss or yarn around the finger near the end of the pencil. Tie a double knot and trim the ends.

4 Cut three different-colored pieces of embroidery floss or yarn, each 28 cm (11 in.) long. Braid them together.

5 To make a bridle, wrap the braided floss around the tip of the finger as shown and tie a knot.

6 Push the finger of the glove down to form the pony's head. Tie the reins of the bridle around the pencil to hold the head in place.

7 Cut two small felt triangles for ears. Fold each ear in half and sew it to the head.

8 Glue on the craft eyes and use the marker to draw nostrils.

Sunset shade

We used sunset colors for this shade, but choose tissue paper to match your room if you like. If your lamp shade is bigger or smaller than the one used here, adjust the number and position of the horses to fit or try making your own silhouettes (page 10)!

YOU WILL NEED

- tissue paper in dark purple, medium purple, light purple, bright pink and yellow
- a white cloth-covered hardback lamp shade, about 25 cm (10 in.) in diameter and 20 cm (8 in.) high
- 6 photocopies of the sunset shade pattern (page 39)
- a spoon, white glue, a small container, a paintbrush, small sharp scissors

1 Tear each color of tissue paper into small pieces.

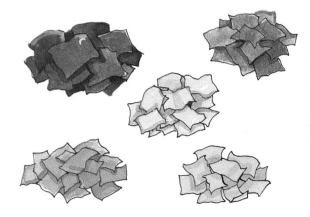

2 Using collage (page 5), start at the top of the lamp shade and brush on some of the glue mixture. Apply the pieces of dark purple tissue, using the brush to smooth them out. Brush glue onto the inside rim of the lamp shade and wrap the tissue paper neatly over the edge.

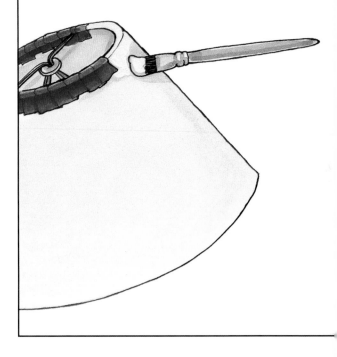

3 Apply several layers of dark purple, then add the medium purple. Continue down the lamp shade, adding light purple pieces next, then pink and finally yellow.

5 Starting with the legs, carefully cut out each horse silhouette. If you cut off any details, you can glue them in place later.

6 Attach the silhouettes along the bottom of the lamp shade by brushing the glue mixture onto the shade and then pressing the horses in place. Brush a layer of glue over the silhouettes and smooth them out. Let the lamp shade dry.

4 To finish, wrap a layer of dark purple pieces over the bottom edge, then let the lamp shade dry.

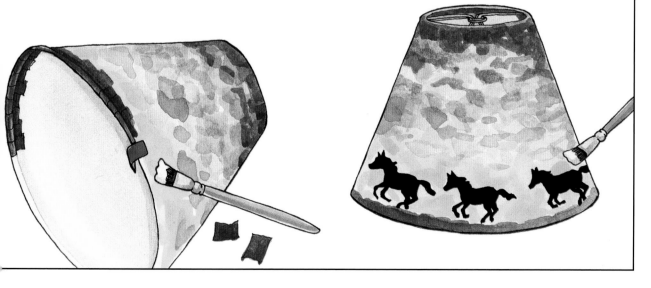

Pony pin

If you'd rather make a necklace, glue a paper clip to the back of the pin at the top and thread a cord or ribbon through it.

YOU WILL NEED

- tracing paper
- a foil container such as a pie plate
- a 13 cm x 13 cm (5 in. x 5 in.) piece of corrugated cardboard
- a ballpoint pen
- tissue paper
- dimensional craft paint (puff paint) in 2 colors
- a brooch pin
- a pencil, scissors, tape
- a spoon, white glue, a small container, paint, a paintbrush

1 Trace the pony pin pattern (page 39) onto the tracing paper.

2 Carefully cut the bottom (or other flat area) out of the foil container and tape your pattern to it.

3 Place the foil and pattern on the cardboard and use the ballpoint pen to trace the design onto the foil. Press firmly with the pen but do not break through the foil. Remove the pattern and cut out the medallion.

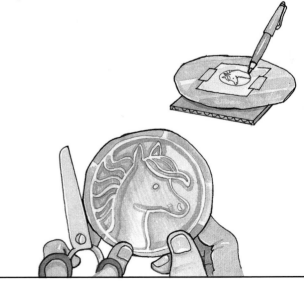

4 Center the medallion on the cardboard and draw a star shape around it. Cut out the cardboard star.

5 Tear the tissue paper into small pieces and use collage (page 5) to cover the entire star. Let it dry.

6 Paint the star and let it dry.

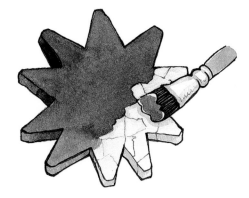

7 Spread glue on the side of the medallion you drew on, then center the medallion on the star.

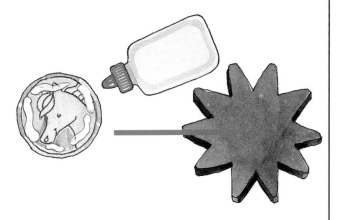

8 Use the dimensional craft paint to outline the medallion and decorate the star. Let it dry.

9 Glue the brooch pin to the back of the star.

Browband cover

Dress up your horse's bridle and make a matching hair scrunchee for yourself.

YOU WILL NEED

- a bridle with a browband
- a piece of fabric about $1\frac{1}{2}$ times the length of the browband and 5 times the width
- a ruler, straight pins, a needle and thread, scissors

1 Place the fabric wrong side down and fold under 1 cm ($\frac{1}{2}$ in.) at each end.

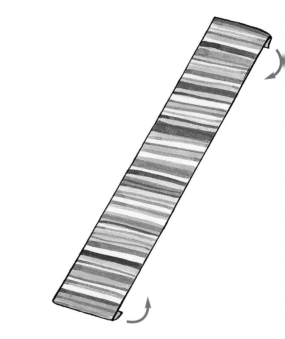

2 Fold the material in half, lining up the long edges. Pin it in place.

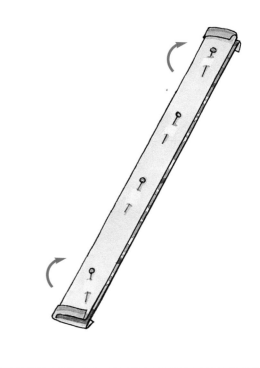

3 Leaving a 1 cm (½ in.) seam, backstitch (page 7) along the edge to make a tube.

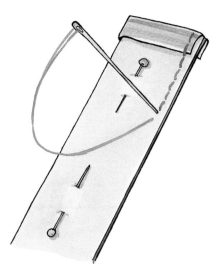

5 Ask an adult to remove the browband from the bridle. Slide the cover onto the browband and re-attach the browband to the bridle. Even out the cover when you put the bridle on your horse.

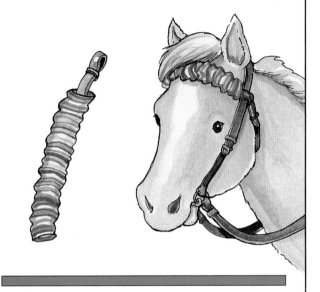

4 Remove the pins and turn the tube right side out.

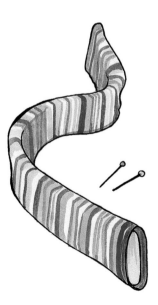

MORE IDEAS

To make a hair scrunchee, sew another fabric tube and use a safety pin to thread a 23 cm (9 in.) piece of 0.5 cm (¼ in.) elastic into it. Knot the ends of the elastic together, tuck one end of the tube inside the other and stitch it closed.

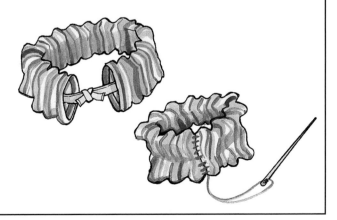

Paddock mirror

*Use your own drawings or silhouettes
(pages 8–11) to decorate this frame.
Or clip pictures from an old horse calendar
or magazines you've finished reading.*

YOU WILL NEED

- a small, rectangular mirror
- corrugated cardboard, one piece 2 times as wide and 2½ times as tall as the mirror, and four 2 cm (¾ in.) wide strips as long as the large piece of cardboard is wide
- a piece of light cardboard the same width and ½ the height of the large piece of corrugated cardboard
- pictures, drawings, silhouettes or photos of horses
- about 7 craft sticks
- 5 to 10 large beads or buttons
- a pencil, a ruler, a utility knife or scissors, duct tape, white glue, paint, a paintbrush

1 For the frame, center the mirror on the large piece of cardboard and trace around it.

2 Remove the mirror and draw a second rectangle inside the first, 0.5 cm (¼ in.) smaller on all sides. Cut out and discard the smaller rectangle.

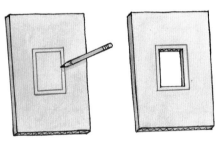

3 Cut a curvy line along the top of the frame. Paint the frame and let it dry.

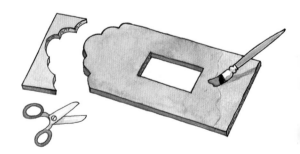

4 Use the duct tape to attach the mirror to the back of the frame.

5 Glue the pictures to the printed side of the light cardboard. Cut around the details and trim the pictures to fit the frame. Glue them in place.

7 To make a fence, glue the craft sticks to the cardboard strips. Paint the fence, let it dry, then glue it to the frame.

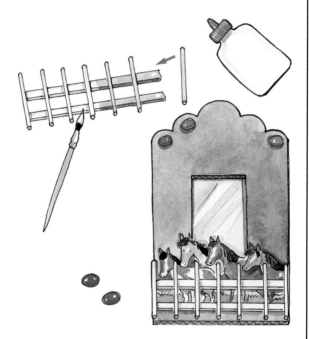

8 Glue the beads or buttons to the frame.

6 Glue two of the cardboard strips together to make a double-layer strip. Repeat with the two remaining strips.

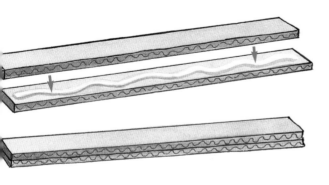

MORE IDEAS

Frame a favorite photo instead of a mirror.

Pony plaque

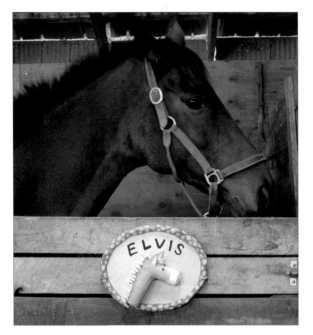

If you don't have a horse and stall, paint your name on the plaque and hang it on your bedroom door!

YOU WILL NEED

- a piece of corrugated cardboard 25 cm x 30 cm (10 in. x 12 in.)
- 2 sheets of newspaper
- 2 toilet tissue tubes
- paper towels
- scraps of felt
- 2 black beads or small buttons
- a pencil, scissors, masking tape
- a spoon, white glue, a small container, paint, a paintbrush

1 For the base of the plaque, draw an oval shape onto the cardboard and cut it out.

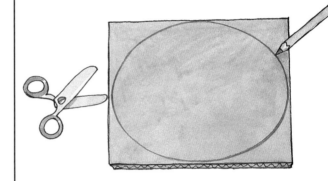

2 Roll and twist each sheet of newspaper into a rope. Tape them around the edge of the base.

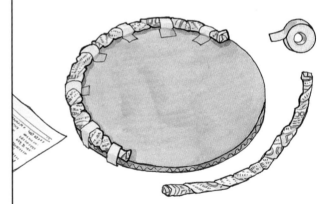

3 Tape the toilet tissue rolls onto the base as shown.

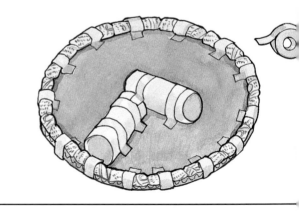

4 Roll half a piece of paper towel into a ball. Stuff the ball into the end of the toilet tissue tube to make a rounded nose shape.

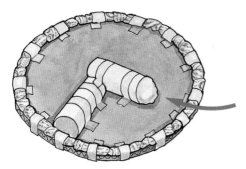

5 Cut ear shapes from scraps of cardboard and tape them in place.

6 Tear several sheets of paper towel into strips. Use collage (page 5) to cover the base and horse in several layers of paper towel. Let the plaque dry.

7 Paint the base and the horse. Paint your horse's name (or yours) across the top of the plaque.

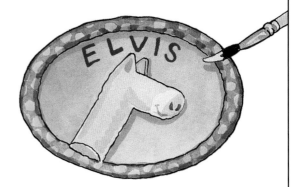

8 For the mane, cut a strip of felt 6.5 cm x 15 cm (2½ in. x 6 in.) long. Cut a fringe along one long edge, then glue the mane to the horse's neck. Cut a fringe on a smaller piece of felt to make the forelock and glue it in place.

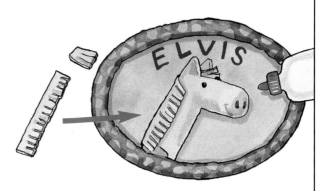

9 Glue on the beads or buttons for eyes.

10 Ask an adult to help you nail the plaque to your horse's stall, or use strong, double-sided tape to attach it to your bedroom door.

Clippity-clop clipboard

How handy to have a few extra horses hanging around the stable or your bedroom!

YOU WILL NEED

- 7 wooden clothespins
- 14 small beads
- 2 pieces of corrugated cardboard, each 14 cm x 52.5 cm (5½ in. x 21 in.)
- a pencil, a ruler, a white colored pencil, white glue, paint, a paintbrush

1 Paint each clothespin to look like a horse's head. When the paint is dry, glue on the beads for eyes.

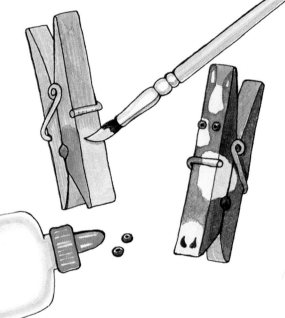

2 Glue the strips of cardboard together to make the base. Let the glue dry.

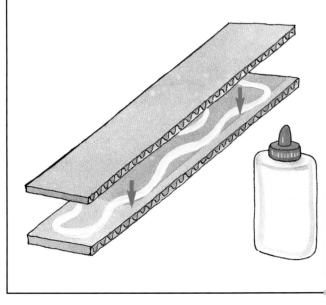

3 Draw a straight line 8 cm (3¼ in.) from the bottom of the base. Paint the area below the line red and above the line blue. Let it dry.

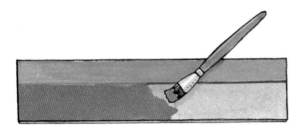

4 Use the white colored pencil to draw a line to divide the red and blue paint.

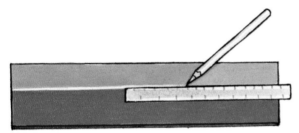

5 Make a colored pencil mark every 7.5 cm (3 in.) along the bottom of the base. You should have six points. Draw a line straight up from each point, then draw a line from corner to corner of each stall door to make an **X**.

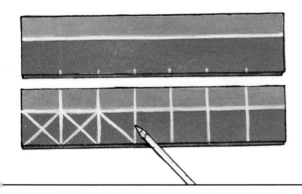

6 Glue a clothespin horse to each door. Let the glue dry, then paint each horse's body.

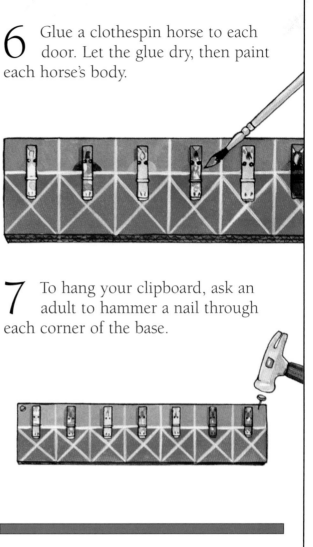

7 To hang your clipboard, ask an adult to hammer a nail through each corner of the base.

MORE IDEAS

String a clothesline across your bedroom wall and use clothespin horses to hang your ribbons or photos on it.

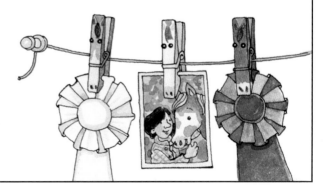

Pasture pillow

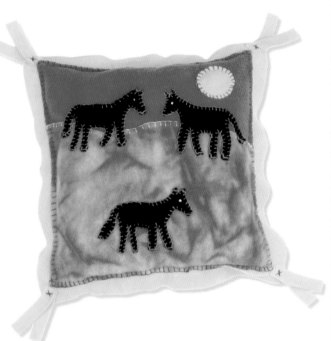

To make a matching wall hanging, sew a second pillow but skip the stuffing!

YOU WILL NEED

- fleece fabric, 1 green piece
25 cm x 35 cm (10 in. x 14 in.), 1 blue piece
35 cm x 35 cm (14 in. x 14 in.), 1 yellow
piece 40 cm x 40 cm (16 in. x 16 in.)
large scraps of black and yellow
- embroidery floss in yellow, blue,
red and white
- tracing paper
- fiberfill stuffing
- scissors, straight pins, a darning needle,
a pencil

1 Cut a curvy line along one long edge of the green fleece. Pin it to the blue fleece, lining up the sides and bottom edge. Blanket-stitch (page 6) along the curve with yellow embroidery floss. This is your pillow front.

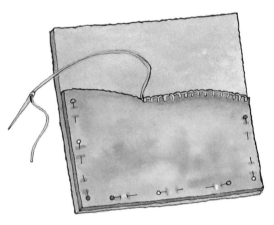

2 Trace or photocopy the pasture pillow pattern (page 39) and pin it to a scrap of black fleece. Cut out the horse shape. Cut the dotted line on the pattern to create legs. Make two more horses in the same way.

3 For a sun, cut a circle of yellow fleece from a scrap. Pin the sun and the horses to the pillow front. Use blue floss to blanket-stitch around each horse and red floss to blanket-stitch around the sun. Remove the pins.

5 Center the pillow front on the yellow square of felt. Pin the pieces together. Starting at one corner, use red floss to blanket-stitch around three sides and halfway along the fourth. Remove the pins.

6 Stuff the pillow with fiberfill stuffing, then blanket-stitch it closed.

4 For the horses' eyes, make several small stitches with the white embroidery floss.

7 From scraps of yellow felt, cut four 2 cm x 18 cm (3/4 in. x 7 in.) strips. Fold each strip in half, and sew one to each corner of the pillow by stitching an **X**.

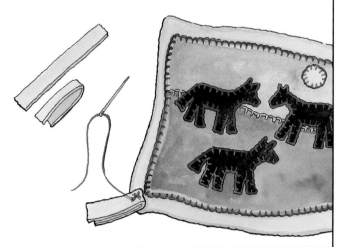

Horsin' around keepsake box

This box is a special place to corral your photos, ribbons and mementos. Use pictures from old magazines or calendars, or photocopy photos of your favorite horses.

YOU WILL NEED

- a 10 cm x 15 cm (4 in. x 6 in.) photo
- a shoebox
- a piece of corrugated cardboard the same size as the box lid
- a piece of light cardboard the same size as the box lid
- a sheet of gift wrap
- horse pictures from magazines or calendars
- masking tape, a pencil, a ruler, a utility knife or scissors
- a spoon, white glue, a small container, a paintbrush

1 To make the frame, tape the photo in the center of the corrugated cardboard and trace around it.

2 Cut two strips of light cardboard as wide as the space at the sides of the photo and as long as the side of the box. Cut a third strip as wide and as long as the space at the bottom of the photo. Set the strips aside.

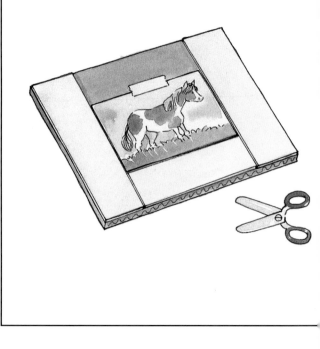

3 Remove the photo from the frame. Inside the rectangle, draw a second rectangle that is 0.5 cm (¼ in.) smaller on all sides. Cut out the smaller rectangle.

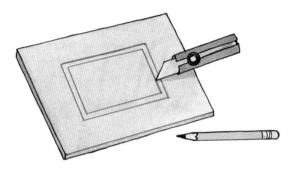

4 Use collage (page 5) to cover the front of the frame with strips of gift wrap, neatly wrapping all edges. Let the frame dry.

5 Collage the bottom of the box and the sides and top edges of the lid in strips of gift wrap. Let the bottom and lid dry.

6 Collage the photos along the bottom edge of the box. Let the box dry.

7 Glue the light cardboard strips to the lid of the box, lining up the outside edges. When they are dry, apply glue to the strips and place the frame on the lid. Set a heavy book on top until the glue dries.

8 Slide the photo into the frame and place the lid on the box.

Blue jean bag

You can sew this bag by hand, or ask an adult to help you use a sewing machine.

YOU WILL NEED

- a pair of old blue jeans
- felt, 1 white piece 20 cm x 20 cm (8 in. x 8 in.), black and brown scraps
- beaded trim, about 60 cm (24 in.) long
- 10 to 12 different colored buttons
- a ballpoint pen, a ruler, scissors, a needle and thread, straight pins, white glue

1 Turn the blue jeans inside out and draw a straight line across the top of the legs. Cut along the line.

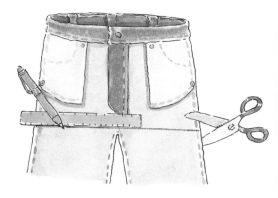

2 Backstitch (page 7) along the bottom edge to make a bag. Turn the bag right side out.

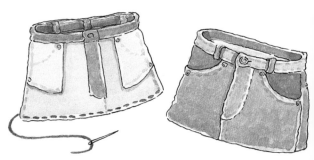

3 To make a shoulder strap, cut a 10 cm (4 in.) wide strip the length of one of the legs.

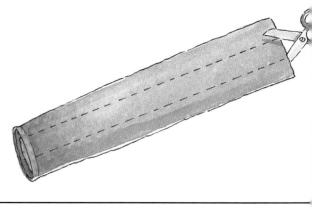

4 Fold the strip in half lengthwise. Fold and pin in 1 cm (½ in.) along each edge. Backstitch along the edge. (If you want a longer shoulder strap, cut, fold and sew a second strap and stitch it to the first.)

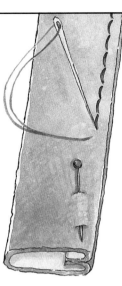

7 Add felt spots and nostrils. Cut fringes along a strip of felt to make a mane. Sew on a button for an eye.

5 Stitch the ends of the strap to the inside of the bag at the waist.

8 Cut 2 pieces of beaded trim as long as the side seams of the bag. Overcast-stitch (page 7) them in place as shown.

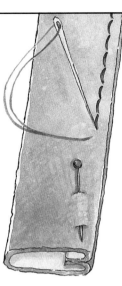

6 Trace or photocopy the blue jean bag pattern (page 40) and pin it to the white piece of felt. Cut out the horse and glue it to the bag.

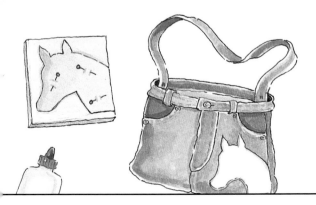

9 Sew the buttons around the waist of the bag.

Bronco bookend

Round up your horse books and magazines and keep them in place with this handy bookend.

YOU WILL NEED

- corrugated cardboard, 2 pieces 13 cm x 30 cm (5 in. x 12 in.), 1 piece 13 cm x 25 cm (5 in. x 10 in.), 1 piece 20 cm x 20 cm (8 in. x 8 in.)
- 2 black beads
- black or brown yarn
- a pencil, a ruler, a utility knife, white glue, scissors, paint, a paintbrush, masking tape

1 On each of the 13 cm x 30 cm (5 in. x 12 in.) pieces of cardboard, draw a line 13 cm (5 in.) from one end. Score along the line and fold the cardboard along the score.

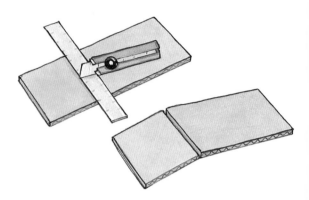

2 To assemble the base, glue the longer sections of each piece together as shown. Let the glue dry.

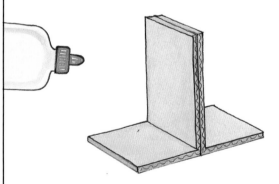

3 Trim the edge to make an arch.

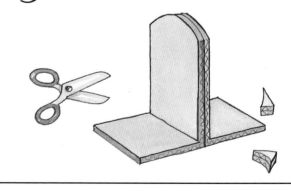

4 Glue the 13 cm x 25 cm (5 in. x 10 in.) piece of cardboard to the bottom of the base. Paint the base and let it dry.

5 Trace or photocopy the bronco bookend pattern (page 40) and tape it to the square of cardboard. Cut out the horse and paint both sides. Glue on the beads for eyes.

6 Center the horse on the base and draw lines where it touches. Set the horse aside and ask an adult to cut along the lines with a utility knife to create two slots.

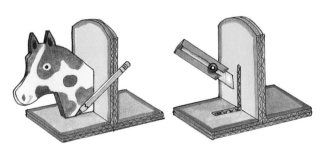

7 Apply glue in the slots and insert the horse. Let it dry.

8 To make the mane and forelock, cut several 20 cm (8 in.) pieces of yarn. Unravel the yarn and glue the pieces in place.

CD stable

This stable is the perfect size for CDs or a collection of small model horses!

YOU WILL NEED

• corrugated cardboard,
1 piece 25 cm x 29 cm (10 in. x 11½ in.),
2 pieces 17 cm x 28 cm (6½ in. x 11 in.),
1 piece 20 cm x 30 cm (8 in. x 12 in.)

• 2 decorative beads

• 2 brass fasteners

• a hair elastic

• a pencil, a ruler, a utility knife or scissors, wide masking tape, white glue, paint, a paintbrush

1 Draw a line 14 cm (5½ in.) from one short side of the 25 cm x 29 cm (10 in. x 11½ in.) piece of cardboard. Score along the line.

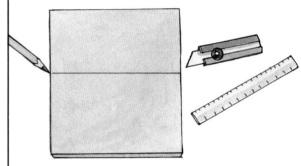

2 On one of the 17 cm x 28 cm (6½ in. x 11 in.) pieces of cardboard, draw a line 13 cm (5 in.) from the left. Score along the line.

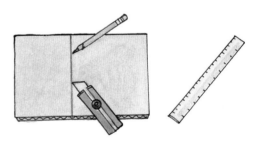

3 On the right side, mark a point 3 cm (1 in.) from the corner. Draw a line to join the point to the end of the score line. Cut along the line.

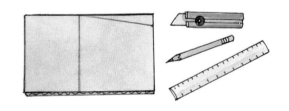

4 Repeat step 2 and step 3 with the second piece of cardboard, but make the score line 13 cm (5 in.) from the right side and mark and make the cut on the left side.

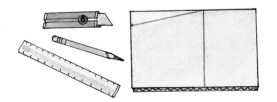

5 Use the tape to attach the piece from step 3 to the left side of the piece from step 1 as shown. Tape the piece from step 4 to the right side.

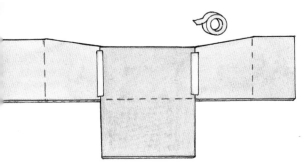

6 Fold up the pieces to make the stable and doors. Tape each side along the bottom.

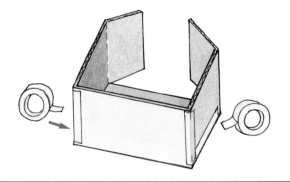

7 Apply glue along the top of the walls. Do not glue the doors. Press the 20 cm x 30 cm (8 in. x 12 in.) piece of cardboard in place to make the roof. Let it dry.

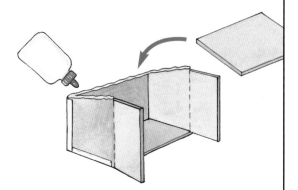

8 Paint the stable, adding details. Cut and glue a horse silhouette (page 10) to each window.

9 On each door, push a brass fastener through a bead and the door. Open the fastener arms to hold the bead in place. Loop the hair elastic over the beads to close the doors.

Sock horse

*Raid the sock drawer and lasso yourself a
herd of wild and woolly horses!*

1 To make the body and hind legs,
flatten one sock and cut out the
shape as shown.

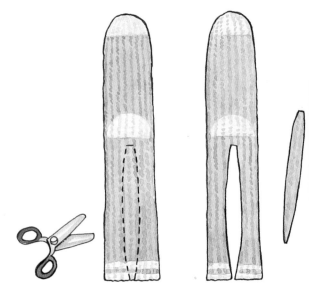

2 Overcast-stitch (page 7) across
the bottom and up one leg
almost to the heel of the sock. Repeat
with the second leg, leaving an
opening at the heel.

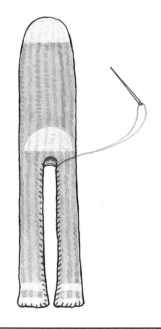

3 Stuff the body, using a pencil to gently push stuffing into the legs. Overcast-stitch the heel closed.

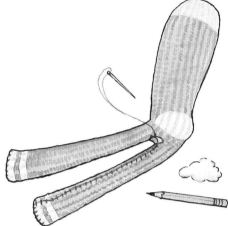

5 Overcast-stitch across the bottom of each arm and up the side. Stuff the arms and overcast-stitch one to each side of the body.

4 Cut the second sock just above the heel. Make arms by cutting out and discarding the center shape from the top half of the sock as shown.

6 For the head, cut the remaining piece of sock just below the heel. Stuff it three-quarters full and tie it off with a piece of yarn. Tie more pieces of yarn to create a forelock.

7 Overcast-stitch the head to the body.

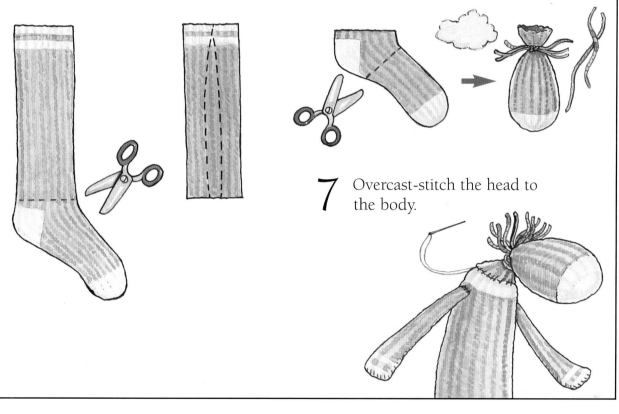

Instructions continue on the next page ☞

8 For ears, trim the heel as shown. Open the heel, press it flat and cut it in half.

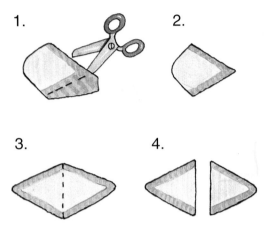

1.

2.

3.

4.

9 Fold one ear over, then starting at the tip, overcast-stitch along the edge.

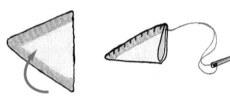

10 Push a small amount of stuffing into the ear, then overcast-stitch it to the head. Repeat with the second ear.

11 For eyes, sew the white buttons in place by passing the needle and thread back and forth through both buttons several times. Pull the thread snug to create an indent around each eye. Sew a black button on top of each white button the same way.

12 Sew the beads on for nostrils.

13 For the tail, cut sixteen 50 cm (20 in.) pieces of yarn. Thread the needle, wrap the thread around the middle of the yarn pieces several times and tie it tightly. Stitch the tail to the horse, tie a knot and trim the thread.

Patterns

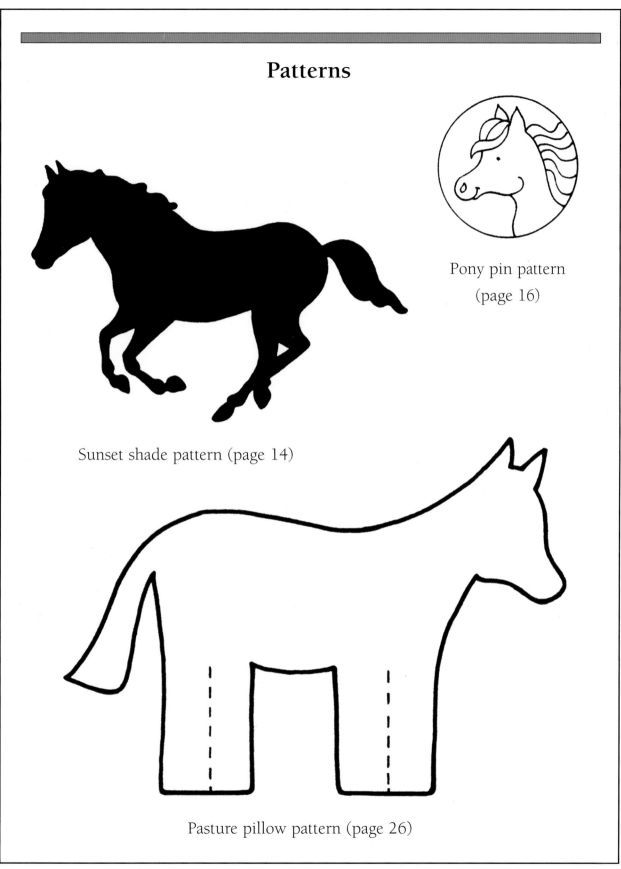

Pony pin pattern
(page 16)

Sunset shade pattern (page 14)

Pasture pillow pattern (page 26)

Horse Crafts © 2006. Published by Kids Can Press Ltd.

Blue jean bag pattern (page 30)
Bronco book end pattern (page 32)

Horse Crafts © 2006. Published by Kids Can Press Ltd.